Our Bodies, Our Shelves: A Collection Of Library Humor

Our Bodies, Our Shelves: A Collection Of Library Humor

Roz Warren

Dude Reads Like A Lady first appeared in the Christian Science Monitor.

Confessions of a Cursing Librarian, Laughing and Looking for Love, You Can't Take Smut With You, What Would Steven Slater Do?, Radical Middle-aged Cake Acceptance, Library Parking For Dummies, War and Peas, I'm Face Blind, Thanks For Trying to Ruin My Day and *Lewd in the Library* first appeared on www.womensvoicesforchange.org.

Librarians! What Are We Hiding and *I'm The Librarian With A Rainbow On Her Wrist* first appeared on www.newsworks.org.

The Librarian and the Porn Star first appeared on www.zestnow.com.

Welcome to Library Work and *The Joys Of Library Work* first appeared on www.phlmetropolis.com.

Freeze! It's the Library Police first appeared on www.broadstreetreview.com

I Am Not A Careful Reader was first published on www.purpleclover.com and appears here with that site's permission.

What Would Steven Slater Do?, Watch Out! Librarians!, and *Library Parking For Dummies* were co-written with Janet Golden and are published here with her permission.

Cover Photo (WHS – 23281) is used with the permission of the Wisconsin Historical Society

Published 2015 by HumorOutcasts Press
Printed in the United States of America

ISBN: 0-692-40646-8
EAN-13: 978-069240646-5

ALSO BY ROZ WARREN

Women's Glib: A Collection of Women's Humor

Men are from Detroit, Women are from Paris: Cartoons by Women About Men

The Best Contemporary Women's Humor

When Cats Talk Back: Cat Cartoons By Women

Women's Glibber: State-Of-The-Art Women's Humor

Women's Lip: Outrageous, Irreverent and Just Plain Hilarious Quotes

Eat, Drink and Remarry: What Women Really Think About Divorce

What Is This Thing Called Sex?

Mothers! Cartoons By Women

Dyke Strippers: Lesbian Cartoonists from A to Z

Revolutionary Laughter: The World of Women Comics

Weenietoons! Women Cartoonists Mock Cocks

For Mark Lowe, First Reader and Best Friend

Contents

Introduction   i

Welcome To Library Work!   1

A Nun Walks Into A Library   7

Librarians! What Are We Hiding?   11

Dude Reads Like A Lady   17

The #@%$ Joy Of Library Work   25

I'm The Librarian With The Rainbow On Her Wrist   31

Confessions of a Cursing Librarian   39

Laughing and Looking for Love   47

Freeze! It's the Library Police!   53

You Can't Take Smut With You   59

Watch Out! Librarians!   65

What Would Steven Slater Do?   71

Radical Middle-aged Cake Acceptance   77

Library Parking For Dummies   83

War and Peas   89

I'm Face Blind. Who The Hell Are You?   95

I Am Not A Careful Reader   103

Thanks for Trying to Ruin My Day!   109

Lewd In The Library   115

The Librarian And The Porn Star   121

Acknowledgements   127

Introduction

A library is a funny place, which makes library work an ideal job for a humor writer. There's inspiration everywhere! Everyone is welcome at my workplace, from local millionaires (mine is an affluent suburb) to the dude who lives in the battered green van in our parking lot. My co-workers and I are all lovable eccentrics, which is to say strong, independent, opinionated middle-aged women.

There are many moments of joy. Singing to toddlers at story time. Sharing the books that have changed our lives. Sharing confidences, too. But there's also plenty of conflict. About paying library fines. About who gets to park in the handicapped space. About whether it's okay to renew a CD that you've already renewed 17 times. These moments can bring out the absolute worst in all of us.

But nobody is allowed to shout.

Meanwhile, the fellow I've nicknamed The Moving Man spends hours, for reasons known only to himself, taking books from the "New Books" section and putting them on the sale table, taking books from the sale table and hiding them in the stacks, and introducing chaos into the magazine racks by shifting all the titles around. There's Supermarket Man, who'll spend hours telling you everything he knows (which is a considerable amount) about every food emporium in the Township.

And, of course, there's the dude who hangs out by the copy machine and warns everyone about the upcoming alien invasion.

You get the picture. A public library is an endlessly fascinating place to work if you enjoy the human comedy, and I totally love my job.

Over a decade ago, I left the practice of law to take a job at my local public library because I was tired of making so damn much money. At least that's the story I tell people. But the truth is more complicated than that.

I was destined, I believe, for library work. My mother was a librarian. But she wanted me to become a lawyer. So I did. However, as every *Star Wars* fan knows, you can't escape your destiny. I grew up with my nose in a book, and spent as much time at the library as I possibly could. In high school, when my friends were skipping school to hang out at the local mall, I skipped school so I could go downtown and spend the afternoon at the main branch of the Detroit Public Library.

The library, apparently, is where I belong.

I've written humor for *The New York Times* and *The Funny Times* about everything under the sun. But the topic I keep returning to is library life. And I'll never run out of material! Just when you think you've seen it all, a patron will say or do something to surprise, flabbergast, delight or totally stump you.

And the responses of my co-workers to all of this are just as entertaining.

The twenty humor pieces in this book (three of which were written with my writing partner Janet Golden) cover everything from what happens when you give a librarian a piece of cake to patron response to the annual *Sports Illustrated* Swimsuit issue to why you can't say "fuck" in the Junior Room.

When I turned 60, I started to think about retiring. Then I came into work to find this memo from one of our sister libraries, posted on the bulletin board:

It has come to our attention that one of our patrons, for reasons known only to himself, placed hundreds of books on hold on his account over the past year, timed all of them to become active today, and then forgot that he'd ever done it. We are looking into this.

What humor writer could possibly walk away from a job that hands you material like this on a daily basis? I'll probably still be behind the circulation desk when I turn 100, eager to see what will happen next.

When I die, just scatter my ashes in the book drop.

Welcome To Library Work!

The week I started working at my suburban Philadelphia library, a scruffy-looking man in his twenties sauntered up to the circulation desk wearing a SHOW ME YOUR BOOBS T-shirt. Although we librarians are expected to strive to meet the needs of our patrons, Eileen and I kept our shirts on. "May I help you?" Eileen asked, deadpan. She checked his books out. Neither of us cracked a smile until he'd left.

Then we looked at each other and broke up.

"Welcome to library work," said Eileen.

Since then, I've seen many stranger things than that in my little library, but I've managed to keep a straight face. Remaining calm, helpful and friendly, no matter what happens, is part of the job. We librarians learn to take it in stride when you wear a tacky T-shirt. Or when you use something wildly inappropriate as a bookmark, then forget to remove it upon returning your book. Deb was checking a book in once when a small foil-wrapped disc dropped out. It was a cherry-flavored condom. "I believe this is yours," she said cheerfully, handing it back to the patron. It was he who flushed the color of his newly returned condom, not Deb.

You've got to learn to go with the flow when you work at a public library. We refuse to lose our cool when patrons bellow at us because we can't locate the book they want, or call us rude names because we won't waive their fines. When the perverts who surf for porn on our computers send lewd photos to the printer behind the circulation desk, we don't flip out. We just roll our eyes and drop the smut in the trash.

Librarians are discrete. You can rely on us not to comment on the titles you take out. When an obese person checks out "Do I Look Fat In This Dress?" we don't say, "Of course you do!" We hold our tongues as we check out books about coping with a cheating spouse or living with cancer. You have no idea how much your librarian knows about you. We're as bad as Santa Claus. We know when you are sleeping. ("What Your Dreams Reveal About You").We know when you're awake. ("Dealing With Insomnia") We know when you've been bad ("How To Regain Her Trust After Your Affair") or good. ("Charitable Gift Giving For Dummies.") Not to worry -- librarians also know how to keep quiet.

When an elderly person dies, his adult children often box up his books and

3

donate them to the library. Among more mundane titles, we'll find a copy of "Sally the Slut" or "Wild Wanton Wives." Not to worry. If you donate Dad's library to us, you can be sure that we'll never phone to say, "we can use everything but your father's profusely annotated copy of the Kama Sutra, although we did find his marginal notations quite intriguing."

Nothing surprises me these days. I didn't know people used currency for bookmarks until I began working here. Now I'm used to checking in a book and having money fall out. I once found a hundred dollar bill in a copy of "Housebreak Your Dog In Seven Days." (Maybe Fido's owner was planning to motivate him with a large cash bribe?)

Recently a book came back in our book drop containing a fabulous home-made book mark. It was a snapshot of a muscular guy in his twenties, stretched out on a sofa, wearing nothing but a big grin. None of us recognized him, but we're all looking forward to the day he strolls into our library. We won't shout "Hey hot stuff -- we've seen you naked!" Instead, we'll step forward with a friendly smile, and ask "How can I help you?"

Then we'll graciously meet his needs. Unless he's wearing a SHOW ME YOUR BOOBS shirt.

A Nun Walks Into A Library

The nun, a petite, grey-haired woman, came up to the circulation desk and handed me a video. It was "Streisand: The Concert."

"I have a little problem," she said. "I purchased this video for our convent at your library last week."

Our patrons often donate used videos to the library. We no longer include videos in our collection, so we put them out for sale.

"I paid a dollar for this," she said.

"And it didn't work?"

"It worked just fine," she said dryly. "That's the problem."

"I don't understand."

"Once a week, my convent screens a movie for all the sisters. It's my job to select the films. We've gotten some great movies from your sale table. Many of the sisters are Streisand fans. So when I saw this, I thought I'd picked a winner."

"A lot of people like Streisand," I said noncommittally. I still didn't know where this was going.

"We all gathered in the convent library. I inserted the video and pressed play. And ----" she leaned forward and lowered her voice, "the screen filled up with naked people!"

"What?"

"We're all sitting there, watching these naked men and women cavorting around on screen, doing…. well, doing some very surprising things. Sister Mary Kate finally asked, 'When's the singing going to start?' Which is when I grabbed that video right out of the player and took a good look at it. On the label it said 'Swedish Erotica!'"

"I'm very sorry, Sister," I said.

I knew what must have happened. Somebody had taken their porn film out of its original box and hidden it in what they thought was a safe place. What could be more innocuous than a Streisand concert? Somehow that very special "Streisand concert" ended up being donated to our library, probably by a family member doing a little spring cleaning.

"I'd like my dollar back, please," said the nun.

Although library policy is to sell videos "as is" and not issue refunds, I handed that dollar right over. Along with a sincere apology. "Please choose another video for your convent's library, free of charge," I told her. "In fact, please take several."

"Thank you," she said. "I believe I will." She headed off to our sale table, an acquisitive gleam in her eye.

From time to time, the image of that room full of nuns watching Swedish erotica pops into my head. And, God help me, it always makes me smile.

Librarians! What Are We Hiding?

I've worked behind the circulation desk of my local public library for 15 years and I love my job. But that job has gone through plenty of changes. When I began, library work was all about the books. These days, while our patrons still check out books, they also come in to use our computers, borrow DVDs and audio books, and learn how to download "content" onto a staggering variety of electronic devices.

Meanwhile, staffing is being cut, and the public encouraged to use our automatic check out system, and to pay their fines and renew their material online.

So are librarians still relevant? Useful? What does being a 21st century librarian mean, really? Who exactly are we? And how does the world see us? I decided to perform a quick Google search and find out.

I typed in the phrase "Librarians are…" and here's how Google's auto-fill completed the thought:

Generals in the war on ignorance
Weird.
Annoying
Novel lovers
Hiding something
Obsolete.
Awesome.
Hot.
Great people.
Heroes every day.

Am I a novel lover? Absolutely. Hot? I'd like to think so. A hero every day? Well, I do feel heroic whenever I am able to intuit where a book that a patron is desperate to read has been mis-shelved, and deliver it safely into her hands.

Still, sensing that I didn't yet have the complete picture, I decided to fine tune my results by running a few more librarian-related questions through my favorite search engines. (Yes, I've got favorite search engines. How librarial is that?)

Being a librarian is…
Great
Stressful
Hard
Boring.

(I'd say it was all of the above.)

A librarian is…
A trained information specialist.
Coming to dinner.
Stacked.

Librarians should…
Read.

13

Rule the internet.
Know.
Know how to spell.

How do librarians…
Choose books?
Use math?
Help the community?
Make money?

Librarians can't…
Save the world.
Buy me love.
Help falling in love.

Why do librarians…
Love their jobs?
Make more money than teachers?
Make less money than garbage collectors?

Librarians need to…
Know about math.
Know about MOOCs..
Know everything.

Librarians can…
Help struggling readers.

14

Change the world.
Work from home.
Have tattoos.

Librarians enjoy…
The silence.
Life.
Shampoo.
The ride.

Sadly, when I typed in: "Your librarian…" the only result I got was:

Hates you.

(Which, it turns out, is the name of one disgruntled librarian's website.)

And finally?

Librarians never…
Die. They just check out.

So what can we conclude? We librarians are awesome. We can help struggling readers. We can have tattoos. We can't help falling in love. But we can (still) help change the world.

15

Is any of this accurate? Who knows? If you want to talk about it, you'll find me behind the circulation desk at the Bala Cynwyd Library.

Unless I'm at the tattoo parlor.

Dude Reads Like A Lady

Yesterday a suit-clad man in his late 50s came up to the circulation desk at the library where I work with a stack of books to check out.

They were all romances.

As he handed me his library card, I waited for the disclaimer. Sure enough, he announced, "These aren't for me. They're for my wife."

"A likely story," I joked. "Don't worry, there's nothing wrong with a dude enjoying the occasional bodice ripper."

"No, really," he insisted, reddening. "She's home with the flu! She sent me to the library with a reading list!"

"It's okay," I said, laughing, "I believe you."

Do men ever check out romances for themselves? In over a decade of library work I've never seen it happen. In spite of the fact that if straight men did read romances, they might learn a few things.

Apparently, they'd rather not.

As a feminist, I'm all in favor of avoiding gender stereotyping. Still, working in a public library has demolished any "Free To Be You and Me" notion I might have had about guys and gals being just the same. When our patrons bring their books to me for check out, there are few surprises.

"Battle Secrets of World War II?" It's a dude.

"I Kissed An Earl?" It's a lady.

Both genders read literary fiction, mysteries and travel books. Nobody of either gender reads poetry anymore.

 And everyone seems to love Stephen King.

But for a certain kind of book, there's absolutely no crossover. No man has ever checked out "Entwined Together" without a disclaimer. And when a woman checks out "Take, Burn or Destroy: A Novel of Navel Adventure," she'll invariably remark "My husband will love this."

Is no woman curious enough about the appeal of naval adventure to fictionally partake?

Not in my library.

Although if she did, she might learn something.

But for our women readers, a book with "naval adventure" in the title is dead in the water. Nor will their husbands or boyfriends go for anything with a half-clad couple embracing on the cover, or the words "love" "desire" or "passion" in the title.

Unless it's "Love Of Mayhem" or "Passion for Tanks, Battles and Explosions."

When a local politician put out a call last year for books to send to front-line troops, Carol and I went through the books on our sale table for titles that would appeal to what we assumed was a group of mostly young, straight guys.

"Battle Earth?"

"Perfect!"

"Nelson's Fighting Cocks?" (Yes, the book really exists.)

"That's a winner!"

We ended up with a selection of macho titles and thrillers, some literary fiction, two Paul Monette classics for the out-and-proud, and (optimistically) a poetry collection.

But we left Debbie Macomber and Jennifer Crusie on the table.

A library patron who overheard us took us to task. "Don't censor the books you send the troops because of your own gender bias," she protested.

"I'm a feminist too," I told her. "But I'm also a realist. Trust me -- sending chick lit to the troops would be a colossal waste of time and postage."

"But if only…"

"We understand your concern," Carol cut in. "But we're trained professionals here. Just let us do our job?"

We sent a bunch of manly titles to the troops and felt just fine about it. If there's a soldier out there who was longing to kick back after a hard day's fighting with a copy of "The Viscount Who Loved Me" all I can say is "I'm sorry."

Will things ever change? They're marketing Easy Bake Ovens to little boys these days, so anything is possible. Maybe we're on the cusp of a Gender Neutral Reading Utopia, a brave new world where women check out "Retreat, Hell!" and men eagerly await the next Julie Garwood.

Would that be a better world? Of course! Opening your mind and expanding your horizons is a good thing. (And I personally plan to tackle "Tank Battle!" as soon as I've finished reading "Crazy for You.")

In the meantime, want to blow your local librarian's mind? If you're female, the next time you hit the library, check out "Take, Burn or Destroy." If you're a dude, bring a batch of romances up to the circulation desk for check out.

With no disclaimer.

(Extra points if you exclaim, "I can't wait to get home, pop open a beer and get lost in "Sins and Scarlet Lace."")

Go ahead. Defy a few gender stereotypes. I dare you. (You might even learn something.)

The #@%# Joy Of Library Work

I've worked behind the circulation desk at a public library for over a decade and I'm happy to report that most of our patrons are pleasant, reasonable people who are a joy to deal with. And then there are the others:

The mother who admonishes her kids, at the top of her lungs, "BE QUIET, YOU LITTLE TURDS!   THIS IS A LIBRARY!"

The man who refuses to pay the overdue fine for returning a DVD late because he didn't enjoy watching it.

The dude we catch trying to steal a bible. (God doesn't want you to steal a bible from your local public library. He wants you to check it out properly and return it on time.)

The guy who approaches the reference librarian, hums a few bars of a song, then asks, "Does the library have that CD?"

The woman who expects us to do her photocopying for her. "You're so much better at it than I am," she coaxes. Better at placing a piece of paper on a sheet of glass and pressing a button? Really?

The man who hollers "Stop pressuring me!" when we announce that the library will be closing in half an hour.

The mother who hurries in the door two minutes before we close and demands that we find all ten books on her son's summer reading list.

The guy who thinks we should let him check out a dozen DVDs even though he doesn't have his library card. Or any other identification. "But you know me," he insists. (No we don't.)

The couple who refuse to pay the overdue fine for the books they forgot to return before they jetted off on a two month luxury European vacation. "We shouldn't have to pay! We *couldn't* return them! We were in Paris!"

The woman who tells us that her car -- out in the parking lot -- won't start and when we offer to call a mechanic, says, "Can't somebody here fix it for me?"

The woman who insists that we refund the money she paid to make a photocopy because the copy has a faint line on it. When we give her the refund, she returns to the machine and photocopies the same page again, resulting in another copy with a faint line in the same place, for which she demands another refund. She keeps

27

doing this until we refuse to give her any more refunds.

The woman who expects us to figure out which book she wants, even though she doesn't know the title or the author, or even what genre it is. "It was on NPR yesterday," she snarls. "Look it up!"

The guy who refuses to pay to replace a missing book because he claims that aliens stole it from the book drop after he returned it there. (You think I'm kidding. Unless you work in a public library.)

The woman who returns a chewed up copy of "The Dog Training System That Never Fails" and insists it was in that condition when she checked it out. When we suggest that maybe her dog did the damage, she says, "I don't have a dog."

Because we librarians are helpful and courteous by nature, we refrain from telling these folks off. Or telling them to get the hell out of our library. Instead, we smile and do what we can to help them. Which, given what we're dealing with, probably calls for its own special guide book. Something like: "When Difficult Patrons Happen to Good Librarians."

Some day I might just write that book.

I'm The Librarian With The Rainbow On Her Wrist

When Henry Ford first began producing the Model T, he was asked what colors it would be available in.

"Any color, so long as it's black," he said.

That's how I feel about my wardrobe. I love to wear dark colors. Check out my closet-- it's 50 shades of grey in there!

I'm a humor writer, and I laugh a lot, but I have a deadpan face. Combine that with my dark garb and I could seem a little dour. But I always wear a rainbow wristband. That small splash of color sends a signal: I'm not as dull as you might think.

It also sends another, more important, signal. I support LGBT rights.

I always have. Maybe it's because when I was young, my father, a psychoanalyst, didn't agree with the then prevailing notion that you were sick if you weren't straight, and counseled his homosexual patients to accept themselves as they were. (One of his favorite patients was a vice cop who had fallen in love -- and was now sharing his life -- with a man he'd arrested in a public bathroom.) Maybe it was because, when the bullies at school tormented me, they often accused me of being "queer." Maybe it was that so many of the writers and artists whose work I loved were gay.

For whatever reason, LGBT rights always seemed like a no-brainer. Alas, other straight folks don't always share my views.

The Rainbow Delegation was started by a young gay man named Matt Mazzei, who grew up in a community so conservative he didn't feel comfortable coming out till he was in his twenties. When he was closeted, he was always hungry for a sign that any of the people around him would be supportive. So after he came out, he created one. A wristband that was a rainbow, a commonly accepted gay symbol.

He gives them away for free.

"I thought that if (LGBT kids) could actually *see* the people who love and accept them," he's explained, " they would no longer feel alone."

Wearing a rainbow bracelet is an easy way to let LGBT folks, especially LGBT kids, know you've got their back. I work in a public library, a place where every kid should feel safe and supported, so when I   heard about Matt's wristbands four years ago, I sent away for one.

When it turned up in the mail a week later, I put it on. I've worn it ever since.

Mostly, I forget that I'm wearing it, but occasionally I'm reminded.

I'm walking down the street in Chelsea. A drag queen strolling toward me sings out, "Gay rights! YEAH!"

A sales clerk at a local pharmacy quietly says, "Love   your   bracelet!" before reaching into her pocket and bringing out her rainbow key chain. Her boss is a bigot, she says, so she's not out at work. "You're family?" she asks.

"Just a friend of the family," I say.

"Even better," she says. "Thanks."

In line to catch a train,   I notice the teen in front of me also wears a   rainbow bracelet. When he glances back and sees mine, his face lights up. "Gay pride! High five!" he calls out. Grinning, the two of us high five.

The good news is that my bracelet has never provoked a hostile or homophobic response. The few comments I've gotten, mostly from curious heterosexuals, have been positive and polite.

And I always get super-friendly service from the gay baristas at my local Starbucks.

But I'm happiest about my bracelet when a teen approaches the circulation desk at the library where I work to check out "Boy Meets Boy" or "The Essential Dykes To Watch Out For." Is it just chance that they've chosen my line? Or did knowing they have my support convince them it was okay to check that particular book out?

Wearing a rainbow isn't the only way I support LGBT rights. I've spent decades writing checks, phoning politicians, signing petitions and speaking out. In 1993, when our son was just four, his father and I brought him along to Washington with us to march (or in his case, be strolled) for gay rights.

Compared with taking action, wearing a wrist band is just a small gesture. Even so, I like knowing that as I go through life, 24/7, I stand for something.

A single friend recently asked, "Aren't you worried that men will think you're gay? What if Mr. Right spots you across a crowded room, then sees your bracelet and thinks you're a lesbian?"

Although I'm now divorced, I'm lucky enough to have a great man in my life. But what if I *were* husband hunting? Would straight guys assume I'm gay? Would I care?

Well, for one thing, I'd want to attract a Mr. Right with enough imagination not to assume I was gay, merely because I'm wearing a rainbow on my wrist.

And *my* Mr. Right wouldn't be put off by a straight woman who visibly supports gay rights.

"If I ever get back into the dating pool, I'm leaving it on," I told my friend. "Sure, it might confuse some guys. But what a great way to screen out the bigots!"

If my life were a sitcom, I'd be husband hunting, and meet an adorable straight guy who also wore a rainbow wristband. Hilarity would ensue as we were drawn to each other, each assuming the other was gay. It would culminate, of course, in a Big Reveal. ("You're not gay? Neither am I!") followed by a fabulous wedding ceremony in which we'd exchange rainbow-hued rings.

Thankfully, my life is not a sitcom. But I did ask Mark what would have happened if I'd been wearing a rainbow bracelet when we met.

"I'm an optimist," he said, "I'd have hoped you were bi."

How long will I continue to wear my bracelet? Until gay kids can trust that everyone, from their teachers at school, to the librarians behind the circulation desk, to every last judge on the Supreme Court, has their back.

That day will be here sooner than you think. I was born in the fifties. I remember the Bad Old Days, when being gay didn't mean you were out and proud. It meant you were mentally ill. Things have changed so much. And they're still changing. Fast. If you want the day when we can all enjoy equal rights to arrive a little faster, you can always wear a rainbow bracelet yourself.

Human Rights are always in fashion.

Confessions of a Cursing Librarian

I recently strained a tendon in my foot, which made walking extremely painful. My podiatrist suggested a cortisone shot.

"This will hurt," he warned, as he angled a gigantic needle toward my foot, "but I think it might alleviate the problem."

When the needle plunged in, and the searing pain hit, I let loose with a stream of profanity that clearly shocked my doctor, a pleasant and amiable fellow, who also happened to be an Orthodox Jew.

I wasn't swearing at him. I was just swearing. But the verbiage I'd unleashed was at odds with my demeanor. I'm a mild-mannered, middle-aged librarian. Up to that moment, I'd been ladylike and well spoken. Nary a "damn" had crossed my lips.

Of course, up to then, he hadn't stuck me with a sharp object.

I am, by nature, well behaved. Growing up in the 60s, my role model for correct behavior was my mother, a woman with exquisite manners. Mom was no aristocrat, just a middle-class Detroit housewife. But she was ladylike to the core, and raised me to be the same.

And a lady didn't swear. Ever.

As a young girl, I never once heard my elegant mother say any of the words I'd just inflicted upon my poor podiatrist.

At most, Mom might say "darn." If truly provoked, she'd allow herself to exclaim "Jesus Christ!" which was always followed by this disclaimer: "I'm a Jew, so I don't believe in him anyway."

My mother wanted to set a good example for her daughters and she did.

Then I became a rebellious teenager and the counterculture kicked in. I didn't want to be ladylike. I wanted to be liberated! I marched against the Vietnam War. I read "Sisterhood is Powerful." I didn't want to be well-behaved. I wanted to challenge authority.

I grew my hair long and wore torn jeans and smoked pot and used profanity.

And if you didn't like it, you could just go *%@ yourself.

Mom was appalled. But perhaps, also, just a little intrigued. I think I was a good influence. By the time I hit my twenties, Mom had loosened up a little. The occasional "damn" crept into her speech. Only, of course, when strictly necessary. But do I believe she enjoyed it.

And why not? As far as I'm concerned, profanity is the spice of life. To this day, at home, and with friends, I love to employ a well-chosen swear word.

Of course, when I got a job in the junior room at my local public library, I had to put a lid on it.

Under no circumstances can you say "fuck" when you're working in a public library.

Especially in the junior room.

Eileen, dropping a heavy reference book on her sandal-clad foot, can only exclaim "Sugar!"

Deb, tripping over an extension cord and falling flat on her face, is allowed to shout "Dang!"

Even when a hotheaded patron, infuriated because I refuse to waive a fine, begins shouting and swearing and calling me nasty names, I'm not allowed to "return fire."

The worst I can say is "I'm so sorry you feel that way."

But when I'm not at the library, I swear. For emphasis. For flavor. To liven up an otherwise dull sentence. To fully express my emotions when Verizon puts me on hold for twenty minutes and then disconnects me.

When it comes to profanity, I lead a double life. On the job, I'm the perfect lady Mom raised me to be.

But inside my own head, and in my own home, and with my close friends, I'm Lenny Bruce. And when I'm really stressed out, the usual profanity gets cranked up a notch. Every other word out of my mouth is a curse word.

If I'm walking to the library, for instance, on a bitterly cold day, and am suddenly blasted by an icy wind, a little mantra made entirely of curse words will start going through my head. "Fuckity-fuckity-fuckity-fuck," I'll chant to myself as I lean into the wind. "Fuckity-fuckity-fuck."

It's best if I can say it aloud, but I don't have to. It calms me just to think it.

Observing my placid demeanor, you'd never in a million years imagine what I'm thinking.

And unless you stick a big needle in me, you probably won't find out.

Although Mom wouldn't approve, the truth is that research backs me up. When you're stressed, a little profanity helps.

A recent study in the journal *Neuroreport* found that people subjected to a painful experience (plunging a hand into cold water) could better endure the pain if they were allowed to swear. The study's author concluded: "I would advise people, if they hurt themselves, to swear."

As a mild-mannered, profanity-loving librarian, how do I feel about this study?

I think it's fucking awesome.

Laughing and Looking for Love

"Sexually, I'm More of a Switzerland" is the second collection of personal ads from *The London Review of Books*, and a more entertaining series of outrageous little paragraphs you will never encounter.

Culled by editor David Rose from among that weekly's more ordinary adverts, these seekers of love are smart and literate (there are footnotes!); their clever, lighthearted prose is equal parts courtship and comedy. Most of these scribes are middle-aged and older, with a few "youngsters" in their thirties

47

weighing in. Which makes perfect sense -- if you regularly read the LRB, chances are you're neither young nor stupid. You're older and wiser, and capable of penning a little gem like:

"Man, 46. Animal in bed. Probably a gnu."

Or beginning an ad with:

"All humans are 99.9% genetically identical, so don't even think of ending any potential relationship begun here with 'I just don't think we have enough in common.'"

These voices are erudite, witty and, frequently self-deprecating. Where the average personal ad is packed with lies, these folks not only refuse to hide their flaws, insecurities and eccentricities -- they lead with them:

"I'm not as high maintenance as my highly polished and impeccably arranged collection of porcelain cats

suggests, but if you touch them, I will kill you."

"Tax-evading, nervous asthmatic (M, 47) seeks woman not unused to hiding under the kitchen table when the doorbell rings."

"Think of every sexual partner you've ever had. I'm nothing like them. Unless you've ever slept with a bulimic German cellist called Elsa."

There's an impressive range of human experience here, from the "angry organic window farmer" and "Scottish historical battle expert and BDSM fetishist" to the "scintillating sex monkey," as well as the more modest "someone who knows how to stop the oven from beeping." What do they seek in a mate? Everything from a "dangerous, tank-top wearing chemist" to "a bloke who doesn't spend 15 hours a day pretending he's a heroic blacksmith killing stuff in some other-dimensional village resembling

Cottingsley, West Yorkshire, circa 1902."

Many of the ads are self-referential:

"I'm placing this ad against my better judgment. But then the last time I listened to my better judgment, it told me the only way to find a well-read articulate man over 45 was to hide in a bin outside his flat until he arrived home from work, then lunge at him as he struggled to put the key in his door."

It's a diverse crowd. Men. Women. Straights. Gays. What they all have in common is the desire to find that special someone. And a good sense of humor.

"I wrote this ad to prove I'm not gay. Man, 29. Not gay. Absolutely not."

"I'm not Edith Wharton, but then this isn't the Riviera."

"Some men can only be loved by their own mother. Not me, I've got Mr.

Snugly Panda. Male, 36 and Mr. Snugly Panda, also 36."

"If I wear a mask, will you call me Batman? Just asking."

Some of the ads are so silly I wondered if the writer was actually looking for love or just clowning around. Probably a little of both. But, really, who cares? If you must look for love with a personal ad, why not have a little fun with it?

"I am Mr. Right! You are Miss Distinct Possibility. Your parents are Mr. and Mrs. Obscenely Rich. Your Uncle is Mr. Expert Tax Lawyer. Your cousin is Ms. Spare Apartment on A Caribbean Hideaway That She Rarely Uses. Your brother is Mr. Can Fix You Up A Fake Passport For A Small Fee."

The ads may be playful, but it's easy to sense, between the lines, a serious longing for connection. When you've laughed your way through this little book, you'll put it back on the shelf hoping that all of these folks will find true love.

Or at the very least, a fabulous fling with a nervous asthmatic or a Scottish historical battle expert.

Freeze! It's the Library Police!

A Texas man was recently arrested for failing to return a GED study guide to his local public library. He'd kept it out for three years.

This is the kind of news story that brings joy to a librarian's heart.

The library where I work just installed a super-expensive state-of-the-art security system that utterly fails to stop anybody from stealing anything, because it beeps, incessantly and seemingly at random, throughout the day.

It beeps like crazy when people *enter* the library.

(When they look at me, confused, I explain, "it's saying 'Welcome to the Library!'")

After fifteen years of library work, this is what I've learned:

(1) Most library patrons are decent, honest, honorable people who wouldn't dream of stealing from us.

(2) The scum who do want to steal from us will do so and can't be stopped.

Within moments of our installing any new security system, the book thieves have figured out how to defeat it. They just tear off the security tag. Or hold a book aloft, just out of the reach of the security sensors, as they leave. Or breeze past the warning signs and zip out the side door. A loud alarm will start caterwauling, but by then they're halfway down the block, confident that a group of indignant middle-aged women with Masters Degrees in Library Science can do little to stop them.

And then, of course, there are people like that Texas library patron, who help themselves to your collection by checking material out and keeping it.

A while back, a woman applied for a library card at my library, received it, then checked out our entire astrology section and carried it off forever.

She ignored all of the polite overdue notices we emailed her. After which she ignored the many fretful mailings the library dunned her with.

Something else I've learned, working at the library? Dunning an unrepentant book thief is a complete waste of postage.

And, of course, she never darkened our doors again. Why would she? She had what she'd come in for.

Those astrology books were hers now.

She was an astrology buff, so maybe she was just doing what that day's Horoscope had told her to do. "You're a Virgo and your moon is in Saturn? This is a good month to steal astrology books from your local public library."

My supervisor, who takes this kind of thing seriously, stewed about our astrology book thief for weeks. She longed to phone her up and say "Shame on you! Return our books this minute. Or else."

But that goes against library policy, so her hands were tied.

This news story out of Texas, though, has inspired us all. Now we have dreams of turning up on our book thief's doorstep.

"Open up, bitch! It's LIBRARY SQUAD."

Library Squad! A group of enraged middle-aged librarians. We're brainy.

We're relentless. We'll hunt you down. We'll never give up.

We know the Dewey Decimal system and we're not afraid to use it.

And we always get our book.

And if you resist? We'll shush you. Permanently.

Alas, unlike the lucky librarians in that Texas library system, we aren't allowed to aggressively pursue our purloined books. Our policy is to ask for them back, nicely. (Sounds like a policy dreamed up by librarians, doesn't it?)

Most libraries dunn their patrons, which we do. Some then turn the matter over to a collection agency. Which, alas, we do not.

Only a very special few library systems go so far as to have their patrons arrested and hauled off to jail. But I don't know a librarian who doesn't wish that her library did.

If we can't arrest these miscreants, I'd settle for being able to shame them on the library's Facebook page. Or establishing a Bad Patrons registry for the worst offenders.

Even gently mocking them via a Twitter feed would help.

But ours is a gentle, kind, library system. We don't actively pursue or publicly shame our patrons. You can help yourself to all the books, magazines, movies and audio books you want. We'll never show up at your door with an arrest warrant.

Go ahead! Check out the entire library and keep it forever! Nothing will happen.

Maybe it's time for me to move to Texas.

You Can't Take Smut With You

Wander through your house and look at the objects you've accumulated during the course of a richly-lived life. The art on your walls. Your crowded book shelf. Your collection of Presidential bobble-heads. Even the clothes in your closet. What you own is an expression of who you are. Like you, it's perfectly unique.

Now imagine that everything has a price tag -- every book, every chair, every salad spinner. Your home is packed with strangers, pawing through your cherished possessions.

"Have you ever seen an uglier pair of shoes? And what about this awful hat?"

"Check out this tacky photo frame. And that hideous mirror! The babe who lived here got more than one visit from the Bad Taste Fairy."

Or perhaps they're saying, "Look at this beautiful vase! What exquisite taste she had. It's a shame she's gone."

When you head off to the Sweet Hereafter, your stuff stays behind.

You'd like to think your children will squabble over who gets your cherished collection of Latvian soup tureens or Marion Winik first editions. And maybe each child will claim a beloved object or two. But then they'll hold an estate sale. A team of pros will come to your house, slap a price tag on everything, open the doors to the public and turn your worldly goods into cold hard cash.

When I was little, my mom loved estate sales. She and I would be waiting on a different front porch every Saturday morning to be first in line when the door opened. When it did, we'd find ourselves in what looked at first glance like an ordinary home -- except that every single thing in it, from the piano bench to the family photo album to the chipped candy dish, had a price tag.

Mom would give me a dollar to spend. While she looked at Oriental rugs and fine furniture, I went for the board games and children's books. I first discovered many of my favorite books on other people's shelves. I still remember taking a worn copy of "Ballet Shoes" from a shelf in a dark, paneled library. I didn't think about that book's owner. I didn't wonder who she was or what that book meant to her. I recognized a good read and paid my dime. Now it would live on *my* book shelf. (It still does.)

These days I work in a busy suburban library, where I'm in charge of the material our patrons donate to us. When somebody dies, their adult children box up their books and bring them in. I never know what I'll find when I open the cartons. A biography of Dorothy Parker. A history of falconry. A Faulkner first edition. Once again, I'm treasure-hunting through other people's possessions. It's easy to get a sense of the person behind each collection. This man loved vintage cars. This woman was crazy about gardening. This man had a strong interest in both butterflies and the Crimean War. This woman hoped to use positive thoughts to cure her cancer. (I hope she did. But the fact that her personal library is now in my hands suggests otherwise.)

You don't want to think about your beloved books being boxed up and handed to strangers. But it could be worse. One of my neighbors, a single man in his seventies, collected poetry. A week after he died, there was a dumpster on his front lawn, and two men were busy tossing poetry books in from an upstairs window.

Mixed in with the books the library receives about understanding classical music or choosing the right puppy is the smut. Badly written books with characters who frolic with a new partner on each page. Sexually explicit comics. Homoerotic photography collections. Victorian erotica reprints. Not to mention a staggering variety of "how to" manuals. That fellow gathering information about butterflies? He was also gathering information about pleasing his partner. Luckily for folks like him, librarians are discrete. When you give us Dad's library, you can rest assured that we won't phone you the next day to say, "We can use everything but your father's profusely annotated copy of the Kama Sutra, although we did find his marginal notations quite intriguing."

What to do with the sex books? We can't add them to our collection and we certainly can't put them out for sale to the public. But a librarian hates to throw out a book. So I've amassed my own collection of the smut our patrons have gifted us with through the years. At our library's "in service" days, I've shared recent acquisitions with my colleagues and we've all enjoyed a good laugh.

The last thing our patrons imagined was that one day their porn stash would inspire shrieks of laughter from a room of librarians. But that's how it goes when you collect something. It's yours right now. But not forever. So cherish and enjoy each possession. But know that every object you love has a life of its own. You never know where it might end up.

Of course, there are worse things than giving a hard-working librarian a good laugh.

Watch Out! Librarians!

We may be a group of mild-mannered, middle-aged women, but when we enter the bar, we strike fear in the hearts of everyone there. We're Team Librarian -- four librarians and a couple of ringers -- and we're here to kick your ass. You usually don't expect trouble from librarians. Nobody ever says, "She's got a Masters degree in Library Science -- watch out!"

Except in the local bars that host trivia games, where we wipe the floor with you.

Trivia games come with different rules and point systems, but they're all designed to extract that precious bit of useless knowledge stored in the back of your brain. The game host asks a question ("In the "Peanuts" comic strip, what did Charlie Brown's dad do for a living?" or "Where do the cops hang out in the Bangles song "Walk Like An Egyptian?") and the competing teams have the length of a song to come up with their best guess, scribble it down and turn it in. (The answers, by the way, are "a barber" and "in the donut shop")

If you can't remember the names of your cousin's kids and you have to run around like a crazy person before every family wedding trying to find out, you're normal. If, however, you can recall the names of Sarah Palin's kids -- Bristol, Willow, Piper, Track and Trig -- at the drop of a hat, then you're ready for pub trivia. (Maybe even for library school.)

The best part of pub trivia is the joy of groupthink. Even team leader Marjorie, who once won $15,000 on Jeopardy, couldn't answer all the questions herself. But when you add in reference librarian Maria, circulation assistants Roz and Trina, and history professor Janet, our favorite ringer, watch out! What could be more fun for a gang of librarians and their pals than putting our heads together to answer a question like "Which state capitals abut salt water?" (Visit the library and look it up if you don't know -- we aren't giving out *all* the answers!)

Sometimes being "of a certain age" is an advantage. "Mr. Green Jeans is the sidekick of what children's television show character?" We knew it was Captain Kangaroo in a nanosecond; the youngsters in the bar came up with answers ranging from Roy Rogers to Sponge Bob. Oh, please! At other times, though, we need some youthful expertise. Questions about Lady Gaga lyrics or video gaming, for instance, are tough. Not to mention the challenge that questions about football stats and the nicknames of baseball pitchers pose for a group of bookish gals. (Don't even get us started on NASCAR...) So we'll recruit a "youngster" (for us, that's under 30) for the team, as well as a guy who has spent decades on the couch watching televised sports. (That's most of them.) Thus augmented, we're unbeatable. Grown men quiver with fear when we take our seats at the local pub trivia hot-spot.

We won't give you a full description of our team. Suffice to say that like Miss America Contestants, we're all lovely and talented. (Plus we know the year the pageant began -- 1921.) Nor will we give you tips about how to avoid paying for your overdue books. (Grow up! Pay the damn fine!) But we'll give you some winning advice.

First, every fact matters. When you read that Jack Kerouac typed at the speed of 100 words a minute, don't just think,

"That's some fast typing." Think: "I'll remember that. Forever." Second, no showing off outside the bar. When friends describe their upcoming European vacation, don't respond, "Did you know there are only two kinds of Europeans whose identity ends with 'ese' -- the Maltese and the Portuguese?" Is it, however, acceptable to shine just a bit. If a friend mentions that she wants to plant moss around the pond, you may ask, "Have you consulted a bryologist?"

Although at times we amaze even ourselves with the factoids we pull from the backs of our brains, Team Librarian doesn't know everything. We once missed the number of bones in the human body, even though we had two doctors on the team. (They redeemed themselves by getting the Lady Gaga question right.) Still, when the night ends we usually have more points than the other teams. We pay the bar tab with our winnings, tip generously, and walk out with a swagger.

True or false: swaggering is taught in library school.

What Would Steven Slater Do?

Once upon a time, flight attendant Steven Slater cursed, grabbed a beer and slid down the evacuation chute of the JetBlue aircraft that was his workplace, and into the hearts of fed-up American workers everywhere. His inspiring (if illegal) escape has given the interior monologue of disgruntled employees a new refrain: "What would Steven Slater do?"

Not all of us who are challenged in our workplaces have an emergency exit slide. And, for the klutzes among us who would have broken a leg on the way down and then been run over by a taxiing plane, not to mention those people who would rather not get either fired or jailed, the exit slide option is not ideal. But we can always dream.

And who has these workplace escape fantasies more often than librarians? Like telemarketers and customer service reps, we must be unfailingly polite. "No, ma'am, I cannot spend two hours working on your crossword puzzle." "Unfortunately, Sir, I am unable to research your family's genealogy back to the stone age." "Sorry sweetie, but I'm not going to correct the many grammatical errors in your Yale application."

Like parking meter agents and cops, we hand out fines and enforce rules that everybody believes in -- till they get caught. "I'm sorry about the tragic death of Gaga, your beloved canary, but I can't waive the fine for that long overdue book." Like teachers, we are poorly paid and asked to do things that aren't really in our job descriptions. "Sure I love kids. That doesn't mean I want to watch yours run amuck while you pop off to the dry cleaners." Like IRS agents, judges, attorneys and the clergy, we hear way more than our fair share of lame excuses.

That's why we librarians were so grateful to Steven Slater for adding a new thrill to our already rich fantasy life. For example:

A young woman sits at a table calmly tearing pages from our copy of the latest issue of *Bride Magazine* and tucking them into her purse.

Watching her from the Circulation Desk, I wonder -- what would Steven Slater do?

If I were Slater, I'd grab the magazine and demand "What's wrong with you? You couldn't make a photocopy? You had to rip up library property? You selfish turd! Besides which -- what kind of messed-up marriage begins with an act of public vandalism? You'll be divorced and miserable within a year, and it will serve you right!"

Instead, I take away the magazine, explaining, "This is library property. I'm afraid I can't let you destroy it."

A woman stands in the middle of our otherwise quiet library blathering away on her cell phone at top volume about her sinus problems.

What would Steven Slater do?

If I were Slater, I'd interrupt her conversation with "What makes you think everyone here wants to hear about your nose? This is a library. Quiet space. Button up or get out." If she made even a peep of protest, I'd grab her phone, march into ladies room and drop it in the toilet.

Instead I tap her on the shoulder and gently ask her to take the call in the vestibule where it won't disturb others.

A patron with a dozen overdue DVDs sneaks them into the library, puts them on the shelf, then pretends to "find" them there. "I returned them weeks ago," he claims. "You didn't check them in properly. Now waive those fines!"

What would Steven Slater do?

If I were Slater, I'd say, "That's a lie and we both know it. Shame on you for trying to cheat the library. Pay up and get the hell out of here before I smack you upside the head with this copy of "Morality for Dummies."

Instead, I curse quietly to myself and waive his fines.

One of these days, a flight attendant will return a stack of overdue books. Handing me the $25 fine, he'll explain: "I'm sorry I couldn't get them back on time. I was in jail because I slid down the exit slide to freedom after the customers finally drove me nuts."

I'll push a secret button. A hidden trap door will spring open. We'll jump in, hurtle down a slide and land gently at the neighborhood pub, where we'll use the $25 to buy a pitcher of beer. As we toast to our escape, I'll look up and notice all three of the library miscreants I just told you about, on their hands and knees, scrubbing the floor.

A librarian can dream, can't she?

Radical Middle-aged Cake Acceptance

I'm processing books in the circulation office of the library where I work when I hear a sudden outcry.

"Oh no!"

"This is dreadful."

"This is just terrible!"

What catastrophe are my co-workers, all middle-aged women, reacting to? Have the library's computers crashed again? Has a letter from an irate patron just been posted on the bulletin board? Is there another new book by Joyce Carol Oates?

Nope. They're talking about cake.

One of our patrons has baked us a lovely chocolate cake, which sits invitingly on the counter in the circulation office. After taking a piece ("I really shouldn't, but...") I return to my work station and continue to eavesdrop as my co-workers respond to this thoughtful gift.

"Oh my God!"

"Uh-oh."

"This is just evil."

You'd think that eating chocolate cake was the worst possible kind of calamity.

"This is treacherous."

"I'm in trouble now."

"Oh dear. Oh dear. Oh dear."

I begin to wonder -- isn't anybody going to say anything   positive?   Such as: "Chocolate cake? How cool is that?" Or "I love cake. I'm having a nice big slice."

Not a chance. By afternoon's end, not a single librarian has had anything nice to say about this unexpected treat. We've gobbled it down.

But have we enjoyed it?

Last week, I helped celebrate my pal Lucy's 40th birthday. As we all sang Happy Birthday, Lucy's husband brought out a beautiful layer cake he'd made from scratch, lavishly decorated by Olivia, their 7-year-old daughter.

Although I try to avoid sweets, I always make an exception for birthday cake. To turn down birthday cake, it seems to me, isn't just rude. It's bad karma.

So I enjoyed a slice. But my pleasure was undercut by the guilt I felt about consuming all those empty calories.

Lucy's other friends also said yes to cake, invariably adding "Just a small slice for me, thanks." or "Just a tiny taste."

But the kids at the party, a gaggle of little girls Olivia's age, had a totally different response. Drawn to that cake like moths to a flame, each child claimed as large a piece as she could, then happily made short work of it.

Seeing cake, they weren't alarmed. They were thrilled.

They were quite a sight, these little girls, beaming, with huge chunks of cake on their plates.

And yet, sometime between now and adulthood, they, too, will stop being delighted by cake and learn to fear it. Rather than taking a big piece and loving it, they'll ask for a tiny slice and beat themselves up about eating it.

Is there a scientific name for this crazy cake phobia? The terror that strikes the hearts of otherwise sane and mature women when offered a delicious dessert? Yes, cake has zero nutritional value. Still, shouldn't a grown woman be able to simply enjoy a piece from time to time?

Listening to my co-workers kvetch about our cake, and remembering how much those little girls loved eating theirs, I resolved that I would try to shed my own fear of delicious pastry and get back in touch with my inner 7-year-old.

Call it Radical Middle-aged Cake Acceptance.

When it comes to cake, I'm going to give myself just two options. Either smile and say "No, thanks." Or have a piece and enjoy it, without ambivalence or guilt, the way I did when I was a kid.

"Cake is not the enemy" is my brand new mantra. (You can try it too. Just repeat after me: "Cake is not dreadful. Cake is delicious.")

Is this an impossible dream?

Invite me to your next party and let's find out.

Library Parking For Dummies

A library patron is a person who uses the library -- to take a toddler to story time, to reserve the novel that every book club in America has decided to read next month, or to pay the whopping replacement fee for that dog training book that Bowser just chewed to pieces.

If you aren't a library patron, please do not park in the library parking lot. Yes, it's free. And it's right in the center of town. But it's a small lot, and we need every space for our patrons. Seems simple, doesn't it? But many of you apparently need a more detailed explanation. So we'll spell it out for you.

The fact that you happen to own a library card does not entitle you to park in our lot if you aren't in fact using our library. Stopping in to use our bathroom before spending the afternoon shopping does not mean you can park here all afternoon. Nor does displaying a library book on your dashboard.

If you're in town to shop, park at the store. If you're in town to pick up your dry cleaning, park at the dry cleaners. We don't have your freshly ironed shirts at the library, so unless you're going to come in and check out a book about ironing, don't park here.

We recently installed a large sign. It didn't help. What part of "THIS PARKING LOT IS FOR LIBRARY PATRONS ONLY" is confusing you?

You fully intend to visit the library after you lunch at the deli? Great! But while you lunch, please park in a metered space outside the deli. Don't park here.

Speaking of which, smuggling your corned beef sandwich into the library to nosh while browsing is not a good idea. Crumbs attract rodents. The only rodent who belongs in this building is Stuart Little. Our reference librarian recently lost twenty pounds on an excruciatingly strict diet, and she can smell a delicious sandwich from across the library. She will eject you. And confiscate your sandwich. So don't even try it.

Yes, that battered green van belongs to a homeless man who spends all day in the library and lives in the van at night. When he parks his van in our lot all day he is hogging that parking space, which is unfortunate. On the other hand he, unlike you, is actually using the library. (The fact that he's using it to take long naps, lock himself in the bathroom to perform his ablutions and plug in to recharge all his battery-operated devices is a separate, if deeply troubling, issue.)

The fact that you are going to the church down the block does not make it okay to park in our lot. God does not want you to park in the library parking lot when you are not using the library. Even if the church lot is full. If you don't believe me, please come in and check out some of our books about religion.

We're happy you gave us a generous donation during our fundraising drive. Thank you! And yet our sign doesn't actually say that it's okay to park here as long as you've recently written the library a large check.

Maybe next time, instead of nabbing the last free space in our lot and then strolling off to shop while blithely ignoring the actual library patrons who are circling the lot trying to find a place to park, you could come inside and check out a book about common courtesy?

If any of this is too nuanced, subtle or complicated for you, feel free to come into the library and ask a librarian. We'll be happy to explain it to you.

While you are doing so? You are welcome to park in our lot.

War and Peas

Some people feel obligated to finish reading every book they start. Once they pick up a book, even if it's hundreds of pages long and makes them want to scream with boredom, they will reach that last page if it kills them.

I am not one of those people. It's not that I don't love books. One reason I work in a library is so I can read any book I want. If it's not in our collection, it can be ordered from outside the system.

I make use of this service so often that the reference librarian in charge of ordering hard-to-find books from other libraries often jokes that she's tempted to hide under her desk when she sees me coming. But even after she's moved heaven and earth to locate a book in some itty bitty library in Bugtussle, Pennsylvania, and it has made the long journey across the state and into my hands, if it doesn't grab me by chapter two, I'm sending it back.

I never feel compelled to finish a book. In fact, I rarely even feel *inclined* to finish a book. I will only continue reading if a book is so great that I *can't* put it down.

A library patron recently told me that I absolutely had to read "The Poisonwood Bible."

"I gave up on it after two chapters," I said.

"It took me fifty pages to get into it," she admitted. "You have to give it a chance."

I did. I gave it twenty minutes of my life. That's all it's going to get.

When I do fall for a book, I fall hard. I read it, and reread it, and recommend it endlessly. I'm the best friend a book could ever have, because I will bring that book scads of new readers. If there's one question you're asked when you work in a library, it's "Can you recommend a good read?"

I'm convinced that I'm personally responsible for several extra print runs of Richard Russo's "Straight Man."

Book clubs are particularly pernicious for the reader who feels compelled to plough through books she can't stand out of a sense of obligation.

A patron recently confided, "I have to read 'Moby Dick' for my book club but it's making me seasick."

"Don't worry," I told her. "I'll help you jump ship."

I printed out a batch of online reviews and she left the library smiling, prepared to discuss the Great White Whale but intending to go right home and curl up with the new Paretsky.

A book has to keep me up till two in the morning turning pages. I refuse to settle for less. The way I look at it, people who suffer to the end of a novel are like people who stay in bad marriages. If the thrill is gone, I want out! Years ago, my ex and I pulled the plug on a twenty-year relationship. Now I'm with a guy who is consistently thrilling, and my ex is happily re-married to the actual love of his life. I call that a happy ending.

Some people disapprove of my ability to jettison a book so quickly. "Once I start reading, I have to finish," they say proudly. I'm guessing these are the same people whose parents made them clean their plates when they were kids.

They probably had to choke down every last pea, even if they hated peas, before they could enjoy dessert.

But you're a grown up now! You can make (and break!) your own rules. If you aren't enjoying your peas, feed them to the dog and have broccoli instead. Even better, toss them in the trash and go right to dessert!

Who cares that you've only read five chapters of "War and Peace?" "Straight Man" is calling to you! Kick Tolstoy under the couch and go with the book you really want. Life is too short (and "War and Peace" is too damn long) to do anything else.

I'm Face Blind. Who The Hell Are You?

You run into someone you know, but she isn't where you'd expect to see her. Your yoga instructor... at the dry cleaners. A member of your book club... at Starbucks. Your mental wheels start to spin. "I know her," you're thinking. "But... who the hell is she?

She recognizes you. She smiles and greets you by name. You return her smile, desperately trying not to let on that you can't place her.

Who the hell is she?   Who the hell knows?

Welcome to my world.

I'm face blind. It's real. There's even a Greek name for it. Prosopagnosia. There's a part of the brain (the fusiform gyrus) that is devoted to facial recognition. If you have prosopagnosia that part of your brain doesn't work.

Which is why, even if we're friends, the next time our paths cross I may breeze right by like I've never seen you before.

Trying to tell one face from another, for the face blind, is like trying to distinguish one rock from another rock.

It can be done. But not easily.

Neurologist Oliver Sacks, ironically, is face blind. So is artist Chuck Close. I believe that I am too, although I have yet to receive an official diagnosis. Why bother? When news stories about Prosopagnosia first began to appear, I was bombarded with emails from friends and family, saying, "Now we know what's wrong with you!"

Brad Pitt recently "came out" as being face blind. (Which means that he and I have something in common besides our sexy good looks and charisma.)

As Brad and I have learned, there is no cure. You just have to cope.

The real problem with being face blind isn't that you can't recognize faces. It's that people expect you to be able to.

If a library patron who has been bringing her kids to my story time for years comes up to the circulation desk to check a book out and I don't recognize her, she doesn't think: "Poor Roz. She must be face blind."

Instead, she's probably thinking: "All these years and she acts like she doesn't know me? That Roz Warren is one rude bitch."

So we face blind folks develop a vast arsenal of ploys and tricks to work around the perils of such social encounters. We learn to identify you by the sound of your voice. Your hair style and color. Your body language. The way you dress. In conversation, we'll try to manipulate you into revealing your identity before you can catch on to the fact that we don't know who you are.

Which isn't to say that we don't still make mistakes. Plenty of them.

When Karen, the mother of two terrific kids I used to baby sit, came into the library recently, I asked, "How are the girls?"

When she just stared at me blankly, I realized she wasn't Karen after all.

Oops.

Then there was the time I foolishly tried to introduce my pal Janet, who'd come into the library to pick up a reserve book, to a neighbor I'd spotted browsing the magazine section.

"Janet, this is my neighbor Deb," I said.

"No I'm not!" "Deb" protested. Because she was actually my neighbor Julie. Both women have short brown hair and live on my block. But Deb is 20 years older (and 30 pounds heavier) than Julie.

Was that embarrassing? Hell yes.

So I try not to assume that I know who you are until you tell me something that nails it. And because I don't know if you're a close friend, a sworn enemy or a total stranger, I greet everyone with a smile.

We face blind people are the friendliest people around. Since we don't know who you are, we'll always approach you with a cheery "Hello!" just to play it safe.

Every day when I'm out walking, a woman I could swear on a stack of Bibles I've never seen before passes me on the street and calls out "Hi Roz!"

Just once, instead of responding with a friendly "Hello!" I'd love to be able to stop and demand "Who the hell are you?"

Or, better yet, require that, out of deference to my prosopagnosia, everyone have the courtesy to wear name tags.

Instead, I'll keep trying to learn to recognize you. And, with time and plenty of effort, I'll probably be able to. But if you change your haircut, a bad cold lowers your voice an octave, or you turn up where I don't expect to see you, I may still draw a blank.

Last week I ran into a library patron at the movies and, for once, oddly, I easily recognized him! "Hi Karl!" I said, with complete confidence that this was Karl and not Bruce or Bob. I was even able to introduce him to my friend Mark without fear of embarrassment.

How did it feel? WONDERFUL. That lost, floundering-around sensation was gone. It gave me a glimpse of what I'd been missing. How splendid and satisfying it would be to go through life actually being able to recognize the people I know.

The next time I see Karl, of course, I'll probably call him Steve and ask how his Chihuahuas are doing.

Yes, there are worse problems to have.

But if they ever discover a cure, I'll be the first in line. Or the second in line, right behind Brad Pitt. Whom I probably won't recognize.

I Am Not A Careful Reader

Some people handle books so tenderly that even after they've read one cover to cover it looks untouched. They turn each page carefully, and always use bookmarks. They refrain from cracking the spine. They never nosh as they read, so the pages aren't dotted with red sauce or spotted with chocolate. And they wouldn't dream of leaving a book lying around where their Yorkie-poo (or their toddler) might nibble the corners.

I am not like that.

When I read a book, I move right in and make myself at home. I dog-ear pages, underline, highlight, and make marginal notes. I'll use the blank pages to make shopping lists or jot down phone numbers. At the ball park, I've been known to use that space to list the opening line-ups of both teams.

By the time I'm through reading a book, you can definitely tell that I've been there.

Of course, I treat library books more carefully than I do my own books. After all, they have to last through many readers. And, as someone who works in a public library, I expect you to do the same. I might dog-ear the pages of the books I check out, but I refrain from writing in them. (Or I'll make lightly penciled notes in the margins, which I'll erase before returning.) Unlike some of our patrons, I don't read library books in the tub. (And if I did, and they fell in, I wouldn't sneak the water-logged book

104

into the book drop and hope nobody noticed.)

Our patrons return library books not only waterlogged, but heavily underlined, stained with last night's supper, gummed by toddlers, colored in by 3-year-olds and chewed up by dogs. (It isn't unusual for our books about puppy training to come back to us with at least a few teeth marks.)

Did you know that there are actually folks who correct -- in ink-- the spelling and grammatical errors they find in their library books? I'm one librarian who welcomes this behavior. The way I see it, these unsung heroes, by maintaining standards of literacy in an age of creeping Twitter-speak, are performing a valuable public service.

I try to return my library books in the same condition they were in when I checked them out. But when it comes to my personal library? I strip off the jacket! I crack the spine! I fold over corners. I underline. I don't hesitate to leave my mark.

I happen to think that makes a book happy. Some of my best relationships have been with books. And who, in a relationship, wants to always be handled with kid gloves? I don't want to remain untouched by a book. Why should the book want to remain untouched by me?

If I were a book, I'd welcome underlining. It's not disrespect. It's affirmation. It's a reader saying "Yes! Thanks! I agree! You rock!"

And folding over a page corner? It doesn't say "I don't care." It says "I'll be back."

My mother, from whom I got my love of reading, never saw eye to eye with me about this. Growing up, whenever she caught me folding over a page corner to mark my place, she'd say, "Use a book mark!" and hand me a slip of paper, a napkin or a file card.

It was a losing battle. To this day, I shun bookmarks. But I'd never think of discouraging you, the library patron, from using them. Not because I'm tender-hearted about page corners. But because those of us who work in public libraries are so entertained by the stuff the reading public uses to mark their places with, then forgets to remove when the book is returned.

Airline tickets. Grocery coupons. Money! (I once found a fifty in a copy of "Get Rich Quick.") Family photos. Nudie photos. A marijuana leaf. A slice of wrapped cheese. Love letters. Once, even, a cherry-flavored condom. (Thankfully, unopened and still in the wrapper.)

Then there was the furious, heart-felt letter written by one of our patrons to her spouse, detailing every despicable thing he'd done during the course of their marriage, which fell out of a just returned copy of "Coping with Infidelity." Was it signed? You bet.

Think about her the next time you're tempted to grab a less than dignified photo of your hubby or a steamy love letter from your sweetie to mark your place in a library book.

Then play it safe and fold over the page corner.

Thanks for Trying to Ruin My Day!

If you work with the public, you're stressed. Unreasonable customers. Demanding bosses. Reduced staffing. I love my job, but the workload is tough and getting tougher. What can we do to keep our spirits up?

Play Customer Appreciation! It's simple. Assign a point value to each annoying thing that happens during a typical work day. When something takes place that stresses you out, you don't scream, quit, or deck the offending customer. You earn valuable points! The first person to reach 100 points gets to slap the next member of the public who gives her attitude, as her co-workers cheer.

No, she doesn't. That's only in the version of the game for folks who've just won the lottery. But what about this -- if you win, you can put your feet up in the staff lounge, pull out your cell and waste twenty minutes gabbing.

Each workplace can draw up its own Aggravation List. In the suburban library where I work, for instance, we'd get points each time a patron goes ballistic about paying a twenty cent fine, or screams at us to check out her movies faster because it's a hot day and the ice cream in the trunk of her Lexis is melting.

The more annoying the incident, the more points. A mom chats blithely on her cell as her toddler heads into the elevator alone, causing you to drop everything to go on a Rescue Mission? Five points! A man with no library card and no ID gets up in your grille because you refuse to let him check out a dozen DVDs? Ten points! And when a patron sneaks an overdue book back onto the shelf, then pretends to "find" it and insists that he returned it last week, don't call him a lying snake! Smile, waive his fine, and award yourself bonus points.

Soon you'll be pushing each other out of the way to help your most difficult customers. The guy who sneers at everything you say? You'll be thrilled to see him. The woman who never says "please" or "thank you?" You'll treasure each encounter. The teenager who calls you a bitch because you ask her to remove her ear buds so you don't have to compete with Taylor Swift when you're trying to talk to her? You'll want to give her a big hug.

The only risk you'll run that you'll be tempted to provoke your nicer customers into behaving like jerks, just to up your score.

"I'm returning this book late, but I'm happy to pay the fine because I love the library," a patron might say to me.

"Are you sure you don't want to scream about it?" I'll plead. "I have 95 points. All I need is 5 more. Go ahead -- vent!"

Customer Appreciation will get you through those moments when you encounter something so unquestionably rude or bizarre that it's hard to believe it's actually happening. A woman approached the circulation desk at the library where I work last week and said, "My car has a flat tire."

"Would you like to use our phone to call Triple A?" I asked.

"Can't someone *here* change my tire?" she asked.

I didn't say. "This is a public library, not a garage." Or comment that when I spent a large chunk of my paycheck on the Eileen Fisher dress I was wearing,

112

"auto mechanic" wasn't exactly the look I was going for.

I just smiled and handed her the phone. If I'd been playing Customer Appreciation, that little encounter would have been a twenty-pointer -- at least!

Sounds like fun, you say. But you're afraid you'd never be able to amass 100 points by the end of a shift?

Are you sure you work with the public?

Lewd In The Library

The *Sports Illustrated* Swimsuit issue just came out, and all over America librarians are flipping through its pages and rolling their eyes.

The swimsuit issue, which isn't actually about swimwear at all, but, is, instead, about young, beautifully shaped female bodies, is the single most stolen item in any public library. Shelve it in your magazine section like any other periodical? It'll vanish. Like magic. Always. But hide it behind the Reference Desk and make your patrons sign it out?

Is that just good sense? Or is it censorship?

Every year, the swimsuit issue gets a bit more lascivious -- the bikinis skimpier, the poses more provocative, the expressions on the models' faces less about "Look at my strong, healthy body!" and more about "Do me! Now! Right here on the beach!"

This year's cover shows three stunning young woman, topless, their backs to the camera, smiling happily at the viewer over their shoulders, their gorgeous rumps more revealed that concealed by itty wisps of fabric.

Is this really what we want to display on our library's magazine rack?

Of course, the collection of my suburban Philadelphia library contains all three books in the *Fifty Shades of Grey* trilogy, and numerous other examples of sexy contemporary "literature." (And the sex scenes in the romances we circulate are hot hot hot.)

We librarians tend to be fans of the First Amendment. I'm a card-carrying member of the ACLU myself. I even subscribe to *Playboy* -- for the articles and interviews, of course.

What I'm saying is that I'm all for pornography.

But there's a time and a place for porn. I wasn't sure this was the time or the place. I'm in charge of processing and then shelving incoming magazines. Before putting this one out on the floor, I decided to consult my supervisor.

Carol and I perused the issue together.

"OMG!" "Would you look at that?" "Yikes!" "Do you even *see* a swimsuit in this picture?" "Gosh!" "I hope her mother never sees that shot."

This was pretty hot stuff.

We were inclined to stash it behind the reference desk, along with the other stuff that patrons like to steal. The

117

Tuesday "Science" section of *The New York Times*. *The Morningstar* weekly stock market updates.

But first, we brought the issue to the head of the library.

Our boss took a look, then said, "Just shelve it. Don't treat it differently than any other magazine. It's no worse than what they can see every day on television."

That woman sure loves the First Amendment.

And, of course, the truth is that we're living in an era where anyone, of any age, can view all the naked tushies they want, whenever they want, online.

"Put a security tag on it, of course," she added. Although we all know how easy it is to remove those tags.

Before I shelved it, my co-workers passed it around. The consensus? We weren't exactly shocked. But we weren't exactly thrilled either.

We're all middle-aged women. Many of us are grandmas. Still, in our heyday, we too were hot chicks. But you can be a hot chick and not want to share that aspect of yourself with the entire world. The kind of young woman who is drawn to library work is rarely the kind of young woman who ends up spilling out of her bikini on the cover of a magazine.

We librarians don't tend to let it all hang out.

Which means that we are, increasingly, at odds with our culture. Modesty? How retro is that? Dignity? Forget about it.

Still, we proudly stand behind the First Amendment. Perhaps, to a fault. And while I wasn't exactly elated about adding that little touch of smarm to our quiet reading room, I went ahead and shelved the swimsuit issue, just like any other magazine.

Within 24 hours, it was gone.

The Librarian And The Porn Star

"I partied with a porn star last Saturday," my co-worker Cat confided during a lull at the circulation desk in the suburban library where we work.

I'm 60. Cat is 30. Despite the age gap, we're workplace pals.

"You partied with a porn star?" I asked. "Tell me more."

"His name is Colby Keller. He invited my friend Jeff to a party at his place in Baltimore, and Jeff brought me along. Jeff didn't tell me that his pal Colby was a porn star. If I'd known, I might have felt uncomfortable or awkward. But I had no preconceptions. So it was like meeting any other really cute guy."

"A really cute guy? Let's take a look."

Did this qualify as a valid library research question? I didn't see why not. So we looked up Keller's blog (www.bigshoediaries.blogspot.com). And.... there he was! A full frontal photo of a very buff dude wearing nothing but a smile. And glasses!

Nothing makes a librarian's heart beat faster than a cute guy in glasses.

"Colby Keller," read the banner at the top of the site. "Colby like cheese. Keller like Helen."

There was nothing unsavory, sad or sleezy-looking about Mr. Keller. He looked happy, fresh-faced and engaging. (And, anatomically, more than qualified for his chosen profession.)

In my youth, I definitely would have partied with him.

"What kind of party was it?" I asked. "Dancing and drugs and debauchery?"

"Actually," said Kat, "it was rather spiritual."

"A spiritual porn star?"

"He had decided to give away all of his possessions," Cat said. "As a kind of spiritual exercise. Or maybe as a conceptual art project. Everyone he'd invited over was supposed to choose a few things they wanted. Then we each took a photo with Colby and the things we'd selected. He's going to post them on his blog."

"That's not what you imagine when you think 'party with a porn star.'"

"I know! That was the cool thing about it."

The library remained quiet, so I was able to devote a few more minutes to researching Mr. Keller. I quickly turned up a Huffington Post interview which called him an "introverted gay porn star." Not only that, but he's apparently quite the intellectual. A sample quote:

"A good part of sex and nearly all of 'love' is a frustrated (through immensely rewarding, if done properly) attempt to experience and share in the subjectivity of others."

Next to these words? A breath-taking shot of the speaker in nothing but the skimpiest of briefs. Sharing his subjectivity would be no trouble at all.

"Was there a mad rush for everybody to grab his stuff?" I asked.

"Not at all," Cat said. "We were all very well behaved."

"So, what did you end up with?"

"A couple of great -- and expensive -- art books, a beautiful vintage 80s dress and a terrific piece of costume jewelry."

"Do you think you'll see him again?"

"I hope so! I gave him a big hug when we left."

In my life I've done my fair share of partying. And I once spent the night with a famous singer-songwriter.

But I've never hugged a porn star.

"If you'd asked if I wanted to party with the star of 'Deep Water Beach Patrol,' 'Cowboys 2,' and 'Splittin Wood,'" Cat said, "I might have hesitated. But since I didn't know about that stuff, meeting Colby wasn't a big deal at all. He's just a great guy."

Do you think that you wouldn't enjoy partying with the star of "Dragon Cumblast?" Or that hot young porn stars can't also be intellectuals? Do you assume that we librarians never party with porn stars?

Don't be so sure.

The only thing I know for certain at age 60? Life is full of surprises.

Acknowledgements

The author wishes to thank: the patrons of the Bala Cynwyd Library, for inspiration, and my library co-workers, for helping me cope with some of that inspiration. My sister Diane, for giving me someone to laugh with (and only occasionally at) during my formative years, which are still ongoing. Lawrence David Blum, my favorite brother-in-law. Mr. Mark Lowe, first reader and best friend. Tom, Amy, Jack and Max, for being the best son, daughter-in-law and grandpuppies a librarian could ever want. Kelly Siderio, who always has my back. Isaac Blum and Amy Blum, for following their aunt into the lucrative, fun-filled field of Writing. Thanks (and treats) to Captain Blum, my personal trainer. A million thanks to Deek, and to Anne Beidler, Rob Haley, Julie Summerfield, Stephen Nelson, Alyssa Dodson, Don Kollisch, Ruthie Nathan, Larry Nathan, Kate Stone, Danny Blum, Barb Straus, Irene Calvo, Nancy Bea Miller, Stella Gabuzda, John Millard and Amy Edelman. Thanks, Hanina Hecker, for making life fun. Thanks, Mike Winerip for making a dream come true by asking me to write for The New York Times. Thanks to amazing editors Donna Cavanagh, Deb Harkins, Ray Lesser, Dianne Morris, Mike Walsh, Shelley Emling, Chris Lombardi, Carla Baranauckas, Sharon Greenthal, Eric Walter, Tom Ferrick, Larry Carlat, Laura Chang, Judy Weightman, Ronna Benjamin, Marjorie Kehe, Dan Rottenberg, Tobi Schwartz-Cassell and Felice Shapiro for taking my humor seriously. Thanks a million, Robin Sindler, for putting me on The Today Show. Thanks, Dr. Patricia Yarberry Allen, for making change happen. Thanks, Wendy Morgan, for my author photo. Thanks to Brock Archer Krahn, for being the world's most exceptional baby, and to Virginia Lee Krahn for being the world's OTHER most exceptional baby, and to their spectacular parents Amy and Nate. Thanks, Steve Klaper, for creating and maintaining my dream website, and Amy Smith, Consulting, for helping me get the word out. Thanks to writing partners Janet Golden, Liz Lowe and Richard Bready, and to writing pals Stacia Friedman, Suzanne Fluhr and Alaina Mabasco. Thank you Joyce Wadler, Nicole

Hollander, Gina Barecca and Marion Winik for encouragement and inspiration. Thanks Katie Bassel for invaluable feedback and support. Finally, I'd like to thank Risa Nye, for this collection's terrific title, and D. J. W. Blum, my trusty circle of fifths consultant.

About the Author:

Roz Warren, "the world's funniest librarian," writes for the *New York Times*, the *Funny Times*, the *Christian Science Monitor*, the *Jewish Forward* and the *Huffington Post*. And she's been featured on the Today Show. (Twice!) Roz is the editor of the ground-breaking Women's Glib humor collections, including titles like *The Best Contemporary Women's Humor, Men Are From Detroit, Women Are From Paris* and *When Cats Talk Back. Our Bodies, Our Shelves* is her thirteenth humor book. Years ago, Roz left the practice of law to take a job at her local public library "because I was tired of making so damn much money." She has no regrets.

You can read more of Roz Warren's work on her website, www.Rosalindwarren.com, connect with her on Facebook at www.facebook.com/writerrozwarren, email her at roswarren@gmail.com or follow her on Twitter @WriterRozWarren. .